Title: Dirt Biking
R.L.: 5.6
PTS: 1.0
TST: 146523

Dirt Biking

The World's Most Remarkable
Dirt Bike Rides and Techniques

by Paul Mason

CAPSTONE PRESS
a capstone imprint

Edge Books are published by
Capstone Press, a Capstone imprint,
151 Good Counsel Drive, P.O. Box 669,
Mankato, Minnesota 56002.
www.capstonepub.com

First published 2011
Copyright © 2011 A & C Black
Publishers Limited

Produced for A & C Black by
Monkey Puzzle Media Ltd,
11 Chanctonbury Road,
Hove BN3 6EL, UK

032011
006117ACF11

The right of Paul Mason to be identified as
the author of this Work has been asserted by
him in accordance with the Copyright, Designs,
and Patents Act 1988.

Library of Congress Cataloging-in-Publication
Data
Mason, Paul.
  Dirt biking : the world's most remarkable dirt
bike rides and techniques / by Paul Mason.
    p. cm. -- (Passport to world sports)
  Includes index.
  ISBN 978-1-4296-6878-1 (library binding)
  1. Trail bikes--Juvenile literature. I. Title.
TL441.M37 2011
  796.63--dc22

2011003478

Editor: Dan Rogers
Design: Mayer Media
Picture research: Lynda Lines

This book is produced using paper that
is made from wood grown in managed,
sustainable forests. It is natural, renewable,
and recyclable. The logging and manufacturing
processes conform to the environmental
regulations of the country of origin.

Picture acknowledgements
Action Images pp. 5 (Studio Milagro/DPPI),
7 top (Studio Milagro/DPPI), 9 (Gregory
Lenormand/DPPI), 16 (Studio Milagro/DPPI),
17 (Studio Milagro/DPPI), 19 (CGW/Reuters),
25 (Miquel Rovira/Reuters), 28–29 (Studio
Milagro/DPPI); Alamy pp. 1 (Mario Moreno),
6–7 (Barry Bland), 13 (Joe Fox), 21 (Mario
Moreno), 26 (Rick Edwards ARPS); Builth Wells
Motocross Practice Track p. 12 top and middle;
Corbis p. 24 (Steve Bardens); GEPA pp. 10–11
(Andreas Pranter), 11 top (M. Oberlaender),
29 top (Felix Roittner); Jopiks Photography
p. 18 (Jonathan Mieze); MPM Images pp.
12 bottom, 14, 22; PA Photos p. 20 (Dragan
Mitrovic/Scanpix); Sierra Nevada Adventures
p. 8; UGC Images pp. 15, 23, 27; Wikimedia
p. 4 (Geraint Otis Warlow). Compass rose
artwork on front cover and inside pages by
iStockphoto. Map artwork by MPM Images.

The front cover shows a rider splashing
through mud at Lake Elsinore, California
(Alamy/Anthony Arendt).

Every effort has been made to contact copyright
holders of material reproduced in this book.
Any omissions will be rectified in subsequent
printings if notice is given to the publishers.

SAFETY ADVICE

Don't attempt any of the
activities or techniques
in this book without the
guidance of a qualified
instructor.

CONTENTS

It's a Revved-Up World

The riders **rev up**, hoping to get a good start when the gate drops. It seems to take forever ... and then you're off! Twenty motorbikes, buzzing down a dirt track, every single one of them hoping to get the **hole shot** ahead of the others.

THE SECRET LANGUAGE OF DIRT BIKING

rev up rev the engine (making it roar loudly)
hole shot reaching the first corner of an MX or SX race first

THE WORLD'S BEST DIRT BIKING

The deafening sound and the smell of the engines at a dirt-bike race is like nothing else. Of course, not everyone rides dirt bikes in races. Some bikers prefer to ride through the woods with a few friends. But the best courses are almost all used for races. If you want to know where to go dirt-bike riding—look for the racetracks! We'll also tell you some of the words only dirt bikers use—their secret language. Armed with all these tips, you'll be welcome at dirt-bike tracks all around the world!

A dirt biker lets off steam at sunset.

PASSPORT TO DIRT BIKING

If you could go anywhere in search of the world's best dirt biking, where would you choose? This book is your passport to the world's top riding spots and to many of the key techniques you'll need when you get there.

If you don't like getting muddy, dirt biking probably isn't the sport for you.

 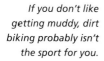

Information: Types of dirt biking

There are lots of different types of dirt-bike events. These are the main ones:

Motocross (MX for short):	Supercross (SX for short):	Enduro:	Endurance racing:
Motocross races are held on a short, outdoor course. The course features banked turns, jumps, and other obstacles.	Supercross is a version of MX that usually happens indoors, in sports stadiums, etc. The jumps are often bigger than in MX.	Enduro races take place outdoors, over a longer course than MX or SX. The riders have to stop at checkpoints at specific times.	Endurance races last days, sometimes weeks. Riders often cross harsh landscapes, such as the Sahara Desert in Africa.

Hawkstone Park

Where better to start your dirt-biking career than the birthplace of MX racing in Britain? Hawkstone Park started life in the 1930s as a hill climb with riders trying to race heavy bikes up steep slopes. After World War II (1939–1945), the first **scrambles** were held here.

RIDING AT HAWKSTONE PARK

Hawkstone Park is one of the most famous tracks in the world. Its biggest feature is an exposed rock face near the top of Hawkstone Hill. A lap around the racetrack also takes you through open ground, some woods, and a sand pit section near the finish (which gets harder the more tired you are).

HAWKSTONE PARK
Location: Shropshire, England
Type of riding: MX track
Difficulty level: 1.5 of 5
Best season: June to September

Riders blast away from the start line at Hawkstone Park.

Tip from a Local

The **whoops** in the woods are a favourite with spectators. But watch out if you're riding them. It's very easy to crash!

THE SECRET LANGUAGE OF DIRT BIKING

scramble early kind of dirt-bike race
whoops tricky section of large bumps

Technical: Dirt-bike clothing

As with any dangerous sport, it is important to wear the right clothes and safety equipment when riding a dirt bike. These are the essentials:

• Helmets and goggles—check that these meet your country's safety standards, and wear as light a helmet as possible. Make sure it fits snugly but is not uncomfortably tight.

• Boots—these protect your feet and lower legs when the bike falls on them. They must fit well and be comfortable, as well as meeting safety standards.

• Body armor and neck braces—buy the best quality, most comfortable of these you can afford, as they are crucial protection in a crash.

Preparing the bike carefully before the race is crucial to success.

ESSENTIAL INFORMATION

Racing here starts in March and finishes in October. Like nearly all MX tracks, Hawkstone rides best when the soil is damp but not waterlogged. The sandstone soil at Hawkstone cuts up badly after it has been raced on all day, so beginners will find things easier earlier in the day.

If you like Hawkstone Park ...

you could also try:
• Mantova, Italy
• Glen Helen, California

Prairie City

Prairie City is home to the famous Hangtown Classic race, which has been running since 1969. That first race happened at Placerville, which in the days of the California Gold Rush had been known as "Hangtown." The race moved to its current location in 1979.

PRAIRIE CITY
Location: California
Type of riding: MX track, general off-road
Difficulty level: 2 of 5
Best season: all year round

RIDING AT PRAIRIE CITY

The Hangtown Classic track is not the only thing happening at Prairie City (although it is open all year for practice). There is also a separate area for dirt bikes and **ATVs**, other off-road areas for 4x4 vehicles, and a go-kart track. There is a huge variety of riding, and riders of most skill levels will find something to suit them.

A rider's-eye view (nearly) of the Hangtown Classic track

ESSENTIAL INFORMATION

Prairie City is open all year. "Red sticker" vehicles, which release a lot of pollution, may not use it between 1 May and 30 September. The northern California weather is rarely extremely hot or cold, but it is a good idea to bring plenty of water. Dirt biking is thirsty work!

Tip from a Local

If you're a beginner, avoid the official Practice Tracks. They are for intermediate and advanced riders.

THE SECRET LANGUAGE OF DIRT BIKING

ATV all-terrain vehicle

footpegs pegs on which the rider stands while in motion

If you like Prairie City ...

you could also try:
• Circuit de Mettet, Belgium
• OCD Motocamp, Canada

Body position on the bike

Most dirt-bike riding is done with the rider standing up on the bike's **footpegs**. Getting this basic position right is a key technique.

1. Stand with the middle of your feet over the pegs. That way, you can still reach the gear and brake levers with your toes.

2. With your knees slightly bent, grip the petrol tank lightly with your legs.

3. Lean forward, with your head over the handlebars and your elbows bent. Your backside will be sticking out a bit.

4. Grip the handlebars well, but keep one or two fingers resting on the brake and clutch levers all the time.

Tackling rough ground is far easier with a good, balanced body position like this.

Erzberg Rodeo

In 2010, 500 riders started the Erzberg Rodeo enduro race. Of those 500, just 15 made it to the end of the course inside the four-hour time limit. This is one tough race—many riders say it's the toughest in the world.

ERZBERG RODEO
Location: Styria, Austria
Type of riding: enduro
Difficulty level: 5 of 5
Held: summer (month varies)

THE RODEO CHALLENGE

The race director says that the idea behind the race was to "bring all the world's best off-road riders here, and present them with an unsolvable challenge." With so few riders managing even to finish, it seems that the organizers have been very successful.

Tip from a Local

People start arriving at the campsites nearby days before the Rodeo actually starts. Get there early if you want to get a good spot!

THE SECRET LANGUAGE OF DIRT BIKING

gravel loose, small stones

Mayhem on the Rodeo course. The rider in orange seems to be going the wrong way.

THE COURSE

The Rodeo course is set in and around the largest open-pit iron-ore mine in central Europe. The "steps" the mine has cut into the steep hillsides present the dirt bikers with their biggest problems. They must get their bikes up jagged rocks, muddy slopes, and sections of **gravel** that are almost vertical. The crowd often helps riders pull their machines up these on ropes!

RODEO CHAMPIONS

The rodeo has been won four times by two riders. Christian Pfeiffer of Germany won in 1996, 1997, 2000, and 2004. In 2007, Tadeusz Blazusiak of Poland started a winning run that continued to the 2010 event.

What kind of crazy racetrack is that? It's the Erzberg Rodeo track, that's what!

Builth Wells

It rains a lot in Wales but, if you don't mind the possibility of getting wet, Builth Wells is a great place to visit. The paths through the mountains and forests have made the town a magnet for mountain-bikers and dirt-bike riders.

RIDING AT BUILTH WELLS

This area offers a change from the glamorous mega-tracks you've been visiting up until now. There are two motocross tracks here, offering challenges for riders of any ability. The main track features jumps, **tabletops**, banked turns, and steep slopes. There is also an enduro course, which takes riders out into the surrounding countryside.

BUILTH WELLS
Location: Powys, Wales
Type of riding: MX tracks, enduro
Difficulty level: 2.5 of 5
Best season: June to September

There are plenty of hills to roar up and down.

Builth Wells — perfect for a dirt-bike ride with your friends

An overview of the Builth Wells tracks

Tip from a Local

If you want to spend more than a day here (and don't mind being woken up by revving bike engines!), there is a campsite at the track.

THE SECRET LANGUAGE OF DIRT BIKING

tabletop jump with a long flat section between the up ramp and the down ramp

ESSENTIAL INFORMATION

The MX tracks are open on Wednesdays and Sundays all year, but they get muddier and harder work outside the summer months. The enduro track is open only during the summer, usually June to September. Riders must wear safety gear, and you can only travel round the course in one direction.

If you like Builth Wells ...

you could also try:
- River's Edge Campground, Louisiana
- Glen Echo Dirt Bike Park, Australia

TECHNIQUE
Cleaning your bike

After a hard day of dirt biking, the last thing you want to do is clean your bike. Thank goodness for jet-washers!

After a day in the mud of Powys, your bike is very likely to need a good clean! A clean, well-oiled bike not only looks nicer, but also works better.

1. Cover the opening of your tailpipe with a plastic bag and rubber band. You don't want water inside it!

2. Jet-wash the bike to get the worst dirt off, then spray it with cleaner. You can get this from bike shops and auto stores. Let the cleaner soak in for a while.

3. Sponge the bike off, and use a soft brush to clean dirt out of all the nooks and crannies.

4. Rinse the bike off. Once it is dry, spray it with silicone spray. Don't spray the seat or gas tank. That makes them slippery and impossible to grip while riding. Don't forget to remove the plastic bag and rubber band from the tailpipe!

Noiretable

The Loire region of France is great for outdoor sports of all kinds. The landscape is a mixture of fields, forests, rocky hillsides, and river valleys. In winter, snows make the region ideal for cross-country skiing. When the snows melt, the dirt bikers come out to play.

NOIRETABLE
Location: Loire, France
Type of riding: enduro
Difficulty level: 3 of 5
Best season: May to September

RIDING AT NOIRETABLE

The town of Noiretable holds one of the races in the **FIM** Enduro World Championship. Riders do three laps of a tough 43.5-mile (70-kilometer) course. They ride up and down sandy slopes, through rock fields and forests, and across streams. Spectators often have to help fallen riders back onto their machines and give them a push to get them going.

This is a course map for the 2010 World Championship event at Noiretable (the course is the blue figure-eight shape).

Tip from a Local

If you are riding in France, make sure your bike is fitted with a proper **muffler**. Otherwise it is illegal.

TECHNIQUE
Cornering

As with all new skills, the best way to learn the art of cornering on a dirt bike is to start slowly. Increase your speed only when you have perfected the technique.

THE SECRET LANGUAGE OF DIRT BIKING

FIM Fédération Internationale de Motocyclisme, the governing body for bike racing

muffler part of the exhaust system that stops the bike sounding too loud

Excellent cornering technique on the Noiretable course

If you like Noiretable ...

you could also try:
- Lovere, Italy
- Hancock, New York

ESSENTIAL INFORMATION

The area around Noiretable is open to non-competition riders. In spring the soil is likely to be damp, though the weather can be cold. In summer the ground is likely to be dry. In autumn fallen leaves add a bit of extra slipperiness to many of the trails.

1. Pick your entry point carefully. Try to enter the corner at a spot from which there is a "clean," obstacle-free route all the way through the bend.

2. Brake as you approach the corner, and shift your body weight forward. Hug the fuel tank with your legs and belly.

3. Lean into the corner, and lift your inside leg (the one closest to the corner) up and forward. Your foot should not touch the ground, but should hover about 12 inches (30 centimeters) above it.

4. Look where you want to go, NOT at obstacles. Your body will naturally steer the bike in that direction.

Campo Grande

Campo Grande is in a part of Brazil whose name is Portuguese for "thick forest of the south." The area's rain forests are very beautiful but also tough for travelling. A dirt bike is an ideal way to get around. Bikes are quick, cheap, and able to deal with mud and flooded roads. No wonder MX is so popular here!

Race action from one of the big bends at Campo Grande

CAMPO GRANDE
- **Location:** Mato Grosso do Sul, Brazil
- **Type of riding:** MX track
- **Difficulty level:** 3 of 5
- **Best season:** dry season (April to September)

RIDING AT CAMPO GRANDE

The MX track at Campo Grande was specially built in 2010, so that the city could host a race in the FIM MX World Championship. This race will happen every year until at least 2014. The track is also open for other races and for practice sessions. Anyone with a dirt bike can turn up and ride.

If you like Campo Grande ...

you could also try:
- Lakewood, Colorado
- Lierop, The Netherlands

ESSENTIAL INFORMATION

Campo Grande is nicknamed "The Brown City" because of its reddish-brown soil—as you'll see when you get to the track. This is not a place to arrive and then realize you left your goggles at home, because the dirt gets everywhere.

THE SECRET LANGUAGE OF DIRT BIKING

lock up skid or slide

wash out slide sideways (usually leading to a crash)

Setting up to brake hard into a corner, this racer has his weight well back and his knees nicely bent.

Tip from a Local

Time your visit to arrive during the *Festa Junina* (Feast of St John) in June. It is a major festival in Campo Grande.

TECHNIQUE
Better braking

Braking harder and faster allows MX racers to stay at top speed longer. Obviously, this is very useful if you're hoping to win races!

1. Stand on your bike in the basic position described on page 9 but with your weight further back.

2. Grip the bike tightly with your knees. This helps to lock your feet on to the footpegs when you are going over bumps.

3. Use the front and rear brakes together. Put them on firmly and smoothly but without **locking up** either wheel.

4. Use the gears to help you slow down as well. Finish your braking before you turn the bike into a corner, or you'll probably **wash out** the front tire.

Enduropale du Touquet

Every February, the little town of Le Touquet is invaded by hundreds of thousands of dirt-bike fans from across Europe. Even the campsites fill up. To camp in northern France in February, these must be hard-core bike fans! They're all here to see the Enduropale.

A CRAZY IDEA—BUT A GREAT ONE!

In 1975, 286 dirt-bike riders took part in the first race across the town's beaches and dunes. Since then, the race has grown bigger and bigger. Today, concerns about the animals and plants of the dunes mean that the race no longer crosses them. Instead, the organizers use earthmovers to build a huge artificial course on the beach. It exists for the race weekend, and then disappears.

ENDUROPALE DU TOUQUET
Location: Pas-de-Calais, France
Type of riding: enduro
Difficulty level: 5 of 5
Held: January

Bombing across the sand at the start of the Enduropale

If you like Enduropale du Touquet ...
go to Le Touquet. There's really nothing else quite like it!

Sometimes, there's a bit of a bottleneck on the course!

SUNDAY RACING

The motorbike races happen on Sunday. The starting signal is given, and a thousand riders all **pin the throttle** at the same moment. They speed off around the first of many laps.

Each 11.1-mile (17.8-kilometer) lap takes the top riders about 10 minutes, and the winner is whoever has done the most laps in three hours. Many riders fail to finish. Crashes cause a lot of damage both to bikes and riders.

Tip from a Local

Make arrangements early if you want to stay in Le Touquet during Enduropale week. Everything gets booked up months in advance.

THE SECRET LANGUAGE OF DIRT BIKING

pin the throttle give the bike maximum gas; go as fast as possible

Uddevalla

Uddevalla must be one of the best-looking motocross tracks in the world. In among the pinewoods, the track snakes and weaves around beneath a rocky slope. This is a favorite spot for spectators at the Uddevalla GP (grand prix)—but you have to get there early to get a space!

UDDEVALLA
Location: Västra Götaland County, Sweden
Type of riding: MX track
Difficulty level: 3 of 5
Best season: May to September

RIDING AT UDDEVALLA

During GP week, a village of tents surrounds the track. Many belong to campers but lots are mobile shops, where you can buy the latest MX gear. The track is much quieter during the rest of the year, giving practicing riders a chance to enjoy its features. These include steep hills, whoops, tabletops, and tight turns.

Tip from a Local

If you're visiting in summer, bring some insect repellent. The mosquitoes can be vicious!

If you like Uddevalla ...

you could also try:
- Jordan River Raceway, Utah
- Westshore Motocross, Canada

Crowds cheer as a rider takes to the skies during a race at Uddevalla.

Sand riding is fun!

THE SECRET LANGUAGE OF DIRT BIKING

psi pounds per square inch, a measure of how hard a tire is pumped up

line route through a corner

TECHNIQUE
Riding on sandy soil

Riders need to make slight changes to their bikes and technique when riding on sand.

• Damp or wet sand is easier to ride (and learn) on than dry sand.

• Let about 10 **psi** of air out of your tires, which will improve their grip.

• When riding, keep your weight further back than usual, to stop the front wheel digging into the sand and pitching you off.

• Stay on the gas! Again, this will help stop the front wheel from digging in.

• To make tight turns, shift your weight forward on to the tank. This lets the back of the bike slip round easily, throwing up a cool-looking spray of sand.

ESSENTIAL INFORMATION
During summer, the sun regularly sets after midnight, and it never gets completely dark. The evenings are cooler, too, making this an ideal time to ride the Uddevalla track. When the track is dry it is faster, and some riders find it easier. Officials do water the surface to help tires cut in and make new **lines**.

Budds Creek

Budds Creek is nestled in the woods of southern Maryland. It is one of the oldest, best-known MX tracks in the United States. It hosts everything from the Motocross of Nations international contest to training days for beginners.

Part of the famous Budds Creek course

BUDDS CREEK
Location: Maryland
Type of riding: MX track
Difficulty level: 3 of 5
Best season: April to May and September to October

RIDING AT BUDDS CREEK

Like other older tracks, Budds Creek uses the natural terrain, instead of relying on obstacles that have been built using earthmovers. Of course, there are still whoops, **stutter bumps**, **off-camber** corners, and other challenges to overcome. The jumps include sections where the best riders leap two or three ramps in one run.

Tip from a Local

The track gets busy at weekends, because it is near Washington, D.C. Go at weekends if you like a crowd, or during the week if you don't.

If you like Budds Creek ...

you could also try:
- Talsarn MX Track, Wales
- Golding Barn Raceway, England

ESSENTIAL INFORMATION

The climate in this part of southern Maryland is usually comfortable for riding. Summers can be very hot, so make sure you drink plenty of water. Although it can be cold in winter, the track stays open all year. Racing starts on the first weekend of the New Year.

THE SECRET LANGUAGE OF DIRT BIKING

stutter bumps rows of small ridges across the track, caused by heavy braking

off camber sloping away from the inside of a bend

A junior Budds Creek racer learning to love the mud

Information: Race flags

During a race, marshals use flags to signal to the riders if there is a problem on the track or with one of the riders. All riders must obey flagged instructions, or they risk being "black flagged"—told to stop riding right away.

Flag color:	Meaning:
Green	Racing as usual.
Blue	You are about to be lapped by a faster rider; move aside.
Black	Pull off the track immediately.
Red	The race has been stopped; return to the start line.
White	One lap to go.
Chequered	The race is over.
Yellow	Accident ahead; slow down, do not overtake, do not jump.

FIM MX World Championship

The FIM World Championship is the top of the MX competition tree. It features the world's best riders in a season-long battle for supremacy. If you don't enjoy watching this, you're never going to enjoy watching any MX event, anywhere!

Huge speed through the jumps at a round of the World Championship in 2005. This course is at Arreton on the Isle of Wight, England.

FIM WORLD MX CHAMPIONSHIP
Location: worldwide
Type of riding: World Championship
Difficulty level: 5 of 5
Held: April to September

THE SECRET LANGUAGE OF DIRT BIKING

cc cubic centimeter, used to measure how big an engine is

two-stroke engine that produces its power two beats at a time

four-stroke engine that produces its power four beats at a time

MOTOCROSS OF NATIONS

The MX World Championship ends with the Motocross of Nations. This is a competition between different countries. Each country enters a team of three riders, and each rider competes in a different class. The classes are MX1, MX2, and Open. To decide the winning country, the scores of each country's three riders are added together.

If you like the FIM World Championship ...

you could also try:
• the AMA Motocross
  Championship

*One of the greatest
MX racers ever, Stefan
Everts of Belgium, in a World
Championship race at
Montperler Circuit in Spain*

RIDING AROUND THE WORLD

The FIM MX World Championship is made up of about 15 different rounds. The riders get points depending on where they come in each race. There are three men's divisions:

• MX1 is the top division, for 250cc two-stroke engines and 450cc four-strokes.

• MX2 is for bikes with 125cc two-stroke or 250cc four-stroke engines

• MX3 for 500cc two-strokes and 650cc four-strokes. There is also a women's championship, run over seven rounds.

Many of the contests are in Europe, but the World Championship has visited North and South America, Japan, and South Africa.

Glen Helen Raceway

In the hills near San Bernardino is one of California's best dirt-biking venues. It might even be one of the best in North America and maybe even the world! The variety of tracks, the warm California climate, and the fantastic racing you can see here all make Glen Helen a dirt biker's paradise.

GLEN HELEN RACEWAY
Location: California
Type of riding: several MX tracks
Difficulty level: 3.5 of 5
Best season: all year round

RIDING AT GLEN HELEN

Whatever kind of MX experience you want, Glen Helen probably has it. There are several different tracks, from the recently designed Pee Wee track for young riders to the international Grand Prix track. One of Glen Helen's key features is its big hills, and the larger circuits are very fast.

Tip from a Local

If you want to camp at the track over the weekend, get there early. It's first-come, first-served, except during the AMA Nationals.

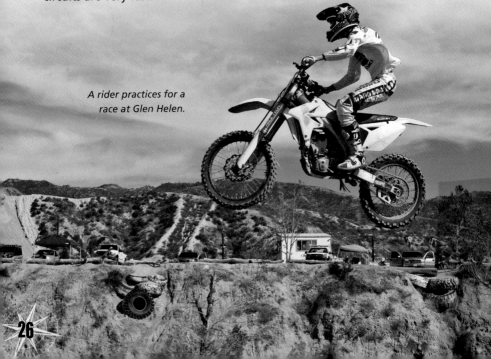

A rider practices for a race at Glen Helen.

If you like Glen Helen ...
you could also try:
• Teutschenthal, Germany
• St Jean d'Angely, France

"Well, I was just riding along, and I saw this nice-looking ramp ... "

TECHNIQUE
Jumps

Jumps are extremely dangerous, so should only be tried by experienced riders or those being taught by a qualified coach.

• Most riders aim to hit the jump straight, standing in the position described on page 9.

• Keep a **steady throttle**, or accelerate very slightly, as you approach the jump. Too much acceleration will make the bike's front wheel lift in the air, which is very dangerous. Slowing down will mean the front wheel dips down.

• Land straight with your feet on the pegs, and bend your knees to absorb some of the impact of the landing. The bike's **suspension** will do most of the work.

• Accelerate just before landing. This helps the bike to carry on in a straight line once the rear wheel hits the ground.

ESSENTIAL INFORMATION
The track is open all year, and racing continues through the winter season. Various tracks are open for practice on different days of the week. It is possible to camp at Glen Helen, and there are places to buy food and drink.

THE SECRET LANGUAGE OF DIRT BIKING

steady throttle constant speed
suspension shock-absorbers attached to the front and rear wheels

27

Gorna Rositza Circuit

Where better to finish your tour of dirt-bike riding than at Gorna Rositza, the best MX track in the world? At least, that what the world's top riders and dirt-biking experts voted this amazing track in 2006 and 2007.

RIDING AT GORNA ROSITZA

Every year, the best riders visit Gorna Rositza for the GP Bulgaria, a round of the FIM World Championship. The motocross track is a combination of long uphills, scary-fast downhill sections, big jumps, and wide sections of track that are perfect for overtaking. This makes for exciting racing, whether you are a rider or a spectator.

GORNA ROSITZA CIRCUIT
Location: Sevlievo, Bulgaria
Type of riding: MX track
Difficulty level: 4.5 of 5
Best season: May to September

If you like Gorna Rositza ...
you could also try:
- Fermo, Italy
- Kegums, Latvia

Riders at Gorna Rositza take to the air like a bunch of turbo-charged jumping beans.

ESSENTIAL INFORMATION

The track is best visited in spring or early summer; the GP is usually held in April. The red-dirt soil will be damp enough for tires to bite, making for some challenging, deeply **rutted** corners. The 1-mile (1.6 kilometer) long circuit is punishing on bikes, so make sure your bike is in top condition.

Tip from a Local

Watch out for the ruts at the bottom of the hill. If you lose your line here you'll be thrown off the bike!

THE SECRET LANGUAGE OF DIRT BIKING

rutted cut into deep, narrow channels

moto single MX or SX race (contests are usually made up of two motos)

TECHNIQUE
Dirt-bike fitness

Controlling a bike in this way demands strength and fitness.

Several tests have found that top-level dirt bikers are among the fittest athletes in the world. During a **moto**, the riders are at maximum effort for about 35 minutes.

Riding regularly is the best training, because it exercises the same muscles that are used during a race. But few people can ride every day, so other types of training can also be used:

• Cross training: activities such as swimming, cycling, or running on soft sand will build up fitness. (Running on hard ground or sidewalks is not a good idea, as it may damage your knees.)

• Strength training in a gym is also important. Being stronger will make it easier for you to handle the 200-pound (91-kilogram) weight of the bike.

Glossary

ATV all-terrain vehicle

cc cubic centimeter, used to measure how big an engine is

FIM Fédération Internationale de Motocyclisme, the governing body for bike racing

footpegs pegs on which the rider stands while in motion

four-stroke engine that produces its power four beats at a time

gravel loose, small stones

hole shot reaching the first corner of an MX or SX race first

line route through a corner

lock up skid or slide

moto single MX or SX race (contests are usually made up of two motos)

muffler part of the exhaust system that stops the bike sounding too loud

off camber sloping away from the inside of a bend

pin the throttle give the bike maximum gas; go as fast as possible

psi pounds per square inch, a measure of how hard a tire is pumped up

rev up rev the engine (making it roar loudly)

rutted cut into deep, narrow channels

scramble early kind of dirt-bike race

steady throttle constant speed

stutter bumps rows of small ridges across the track, caused by heavy braking

suspension shock-absorbers attached to the front and rear wheels

tabletop jump with a long flat section between the up ramp and the down ramp

two-stroke engine that produces its power two beats at a time

wash out slide sideways (usually leading to a crash)

whoops tricky section of large bumps

OTHER WORDS DIRT BIKERS USE

bus stop slow, first-gear corner

case it land on top of a jump, rather than on the down slope

dump the clutch release the clutch quickly at high revs, to make a fast getaway

lapper slow rider who is being overtaken by the leaders

on the box finish in the top three (so that you get to stand on the podium or "box")

squid bad or slow rider

Finding Out More

THE INTERNET

FactHound offers a safe, fun way to find Internet sites related to this book. All of the sites on FactHound have been researched by our staff.

Here's all you do:
Visit www.facthound.com
FactHound will fetch the best sites for you!

BOOKS

INFORMATION BOOKS

Extreme Motorcycle Racing (Extreme Adventures!) Clive Gifford (Capstone Press, 2010)

Motocross (Racing Mania) Bryan Stealey (Marshall Cavendish Benchmark, 2010)

Moto X (Record Breakers) Blaine Wiseman (Weigl, 2011)

FICTION

Dirt Bike Daredevils Pam Withers (Walrus Books, 2006)
The adventures of Jake and Peter, 15-year-old trail guides for a dirt-bike outfit in Washington state.

MAGAZINE

Dirt Bike
Both the magazine and its website have up-to-date news on race results, interviews with riders, advice on technique, and much more. Competition coverage focuses on the AMA Championship and its riders.

Index